Dollar Store Deals Cookbook

I0170938

Meranda Hendricks & Colleen Timko

CONTENTS

ACKNOWLEDGMENTS

The Hound Hut's Colleen Timko and Meranda Hendricks would like to thank their families, friends, and loyal customers who have been there from the very beginning encouraging them every step of the way!

1 APPETIZERS

Black Bean Dip

15 -16 oz can refried beans

4 oz sharp cheddar cheese, shredded

1 c picante sauce

black olives, sliced (optional)

In a small to medium saucepan, mix together all ingredients.

Cook on low heat, stirring occasionally, until cheese is melted

and bean dip is heated through. (Have also made it in the microwave)

 Top with sliced black olives.

May double ingredients for larger portions. Cooks well in a

Crock-pot on low heat.

Buffalo Chicken Dip

16 oz Cream Cheese

8 oz Hot Sauce

2 Cups Canned Chicken (drain well)

1 Cup shredded Cheddar Cheese

12 oz bottle ranch dressing

In bowl mix cream cheese and hot sauce. Microwave until melted. Stir and

Add chicken, dressing and cheddar.

Put all into a baking dish, top with more cheese if desired!

Bake at 350 degrees for 30 min.

Serve with crackers, tortillas, Fritos.

Chili Tortilla Bake

2 cans (15 oz. each) chili with beans

5 Hot dogs

5 corn tortillas (6 inch)

1/2 cup Shredded Cheddar Cheese

HEAT oven to 425ºF.

SPREAD chili onto bottom of 8-inch square baking dish.

PLACE 1 wiener on each tortilla; roll up. Place, seam-sides down, over chili. Sprinkle with cheese; cover.

BAKE 25 min. or until wieners are heated through and cheese is melted

Orange Marmalade Meatballs

2 pounds fully cooked frozen meatballs

1 bottle (16-ounce) Catalina salad dressing

1 cup orange marmalade

3 tablespoons Worcestershire sauce

1/2 teaspoon red pepper flakes

Place frozen meatballs in the insert of a slow cooker. In a bowl, stir to combine the remaining ingredients. Pour over meatballs and stir to coat. Cook on high setting for 2 to 3 hours.

2 CONDIMENTS

Cheese Sauce for Mac'n Cheese, Broccoli, Cauliflower or any Vegetable

Shake together in a container:

8 oz. milk and 2 tbsp. flour, pour into sauce pan

Add: 8 oz. processed cheese cut into small pieces and 2 tablespoons margarine

Bring to a boil over medium heat while stirring constantly.

Ingredients can be altered in amount to make sauce thicker or thinner.

Cole Slaw, Potato Salad or Macaroni Salad Dressing

1 1/2 cups mayonnaise

2 tablespoons lemon juice

2 tablespoons sugar

1/2 teaspoon salt

1/2 cup evaporated milk

1/4 teaspoon white pepper (optional)

Recipe enough for average meal dish. Amounts can be increased and varied according to taste.

Jackson Salad Dressing

If you have a head of lettuce and need to make a good dressing!

2 hard boiled eggs chopped up

1/3 Cup Oil

3 tbs vinegar

1 tsp salt

½ tsp sugar

1/8 tsp pepper

Place all of these ingredients into a jar. An old mayo jar works great!

Cover tightly and shake well. Refrigerate and pour over lettuce and toss when ready to serve.

BBQ Sauce For Meatballs

1 ½ cup ketchup

½ TBS mustard

1/ ½ TBS Vinegar

1 Cup Brown Sugar

1 ½ TBS Worcestershire Sauce

Mix all ingredients and pour over cooked meatballs.

Heat throughly- good in crockpot

3 BREAD

Cheesy Biscuits

2 cups Buttermilk Baking mix

1/4 teaspoon garlic powder

1/4 cup firm butter or margarine

2/3 cup milk

1/2 cup shredded Cheddar cheese (2 oz)

3 eggs

Garlic-Butter Topping

1/4 cup butter or margarine, melted

1/4 teaspoon garlic powder

Heat oven to 425°F. In medium bowl, combine Buttermilk Baking mix and 1/4 teaspoon garlic powder. Cut in 1/4 cup butter, using pastry blender or fork, until mixture looks like coarse crumbs. Stir in milk, cheese and eggs until soft dough forms.

Drop dough by 10 spoonfuls onto ungreased cookie sheet.

Bake 8 to 10 minutes or until light golden brown. Mix 1/4 cup melted butter and 1/4 teaspoon garlic powder; brush on warm biscuits before removing from cookie sheet. Serve warm.

Southern Corn Bread Recipe

1 cup self-rising cornmeal*

1/2 teaspoon baking soda

1/4 teaspoon salt

1 1/2 cups shredded cheddar cheese

1/2 cup chopped onion

1 cup milk

3 Tbsp bacon drippings (warmed to liquid)

1 teaspoon garlic powder

2 eggs, beaten

3/4 cup of cooked corn, either fresh, defrosted frozen corn, or drained from a can

*You can make your own self rising cornmeal easily. 1 cup of self-rising cornmeal is equivalent to 1 Tbsp of baking powder, 1/2 teaspoon of salt, and 1 cup minus 1 Tbsp of cornmeal.

Preheat oven to 350°F.

Combine cornmeal, soda and salt. Add remaining ingredients, stirring just until dry ingredients are moistened.

Spoon into a greased 10-inch cast-iron skillet. Bake for 45 minutes or until golden brown.

Cherry Pecan Bread

¾ cup sugar

½ cup butter or margarine

2 eggs

2 cups flour

1 tsp. baking soda

½ tsp. salt

1 cup buttermilk

1 cup chopped pecans

11 oz. jar maraschino cherries, drained and chopped. Reserve juice for glaze.

1 tsp. vanilla

Glaze:

2 ½ Tbsp. butter or margarine

1 cup powdered sugar.

¾ tsp. vanilla

2-3 Tbsp. reserved cherry juice. Heated.

Cream together sugar, butter, and eggs until light and fluffy. Sift together flour, baking soda, and salt. Add alternately with buttermilk to creamed mixture. Stir in pecans, cherries, and vanilla. Pour batter into a well greased, full sized loaf pan. For glaze: melt butter. Blend in sugar and vanilla. Stir in juice, 1 tablespoon at a time, until glaze is of proper consistency.

Corn Fritters Recipe

1 1/3 cups buttermilk baking mix

1 1/2 teaspoons baking powder

1 (14.75 ounce) can cream-style corn

1 egg, beaten

1 cup vegetable oil

1 1/2 cups maple syrup

In a medium mixing bowl, sift together baking mix and baking powder.

In a small mixing bowl, combine corn and egg.

Combine egg and flour mixture, stir gently.

Heat oil in large skillet over medium heat.

Drop batter by tablespoonfuls into hot oil one layer at a time.

Fry for 2 minutes on each side or until golden brown.

Drain fritters on a paper towel.

Serve immediately syrup.

Raisin Loaf

1 ½ cups raisins

2 cups boiling water

2 tsp. baking soda

½ cup shortening

2 cups sugar

3 eggs

4 cups flour

½ tsp. salt

1 tsp. vanilla

½ cup chopped walnuts

Combine raisins, boiling water, and baking soda. Set aside for 1 hour.

Cream together shortening and sugar. Add eggs and beat well. Add flour and salt alternately with raisin mixture to creamed mixture.

Add vanilla and nuts and stir well.

Pour into four small greased bread pans (3 ½ x 7 ¼)

Bake at 350* for 40 – 45 minutes.

4 BREAKFASTS

Baked French Toast

4 slices Texas toast bread

1/2 c milk

2 eggs

11/2 T sugar

3/4 t cinnamon, ground

Preheat oven to 400 degrees. Spray baking pan with non-stick

Spray. In a large shallow bowl, beat eggs and milk until frothy.

Submerge bread into egg and milk until well coated. Place

bread on baking pan. Sprinkle each piece of bread with

cinnamon and sugar. Place in oven and bake for 8 minutes.

Turn over bread and bake for another 5 minutes or until well

browned on top. Serve with syrup of choice

Brunch Egg Breakfast Casserole

6 eggs, beaten

6 slices bacon, cooked and crumbled

2 cups unseasoned croutons

1 1/2 cup shredded cheddar cheese

2 1/2 cups milk

1/2 teaspoon mustard

1/8 teaspoon onion powder

1/2 teaspoon salt

1 dash pepper

Place croutons and cheese in the bottom of a greased 9x13 pan.

Combine eggs, milk and seasonings; pour into baking dish.

Sprinkle with bacon.

Bake at 325 until set (55-65 min). Serve immediately.

Chocolate Marshmallow Punch

3 12 oz. cans evaporated milk

2 cups chocolate syrup

2 cups water

12 large marshmallows

1 Tbsp. vanilla

Grated chocolate

Mini marshmallows

In large saucepan mix together milk, chocolate syrup, water, and 12 large marshmallows. Heat over medium heat, stirring until marshmallows are melted. Stir in vanilla.

Pour into cups. Garnish with marshmallows and grated chocolate. Serve

Pecan Coffee Cake

<u>Coffee Cake:</u>

½ cup margarine

1 cup sugar

2 eggs

1 tsp. vanilla

1 cup sour cream

1 ½ cups flour

1 tsp. baking soda

<u>Topping:</u>

½ cup white sugar

½ cup chopped pecans

2 tsp. cinnamon

To prepare cake cream together margarine and sugar. Beat in eggs and mix well. Add vanilla, sour cream, flour and baking soda. Pour ½ of batter into greased and floured 8" square baking pan.

Mix together all topping ingredients. Pour ½ of topping over batter in pan. Spoon on remaining batter and sprinkle and remaining topping.

Bake at 350 for 30 – 35 minutes.

Sour Cream Pancake

½ tsp. baking soda

1 cup sour cream

2 eggs, separated

2 Tbsp. sugar

1 tsp. salt

½ cup sifted four

Stir baking soda into sour cream. Set aside. Beat egg whites until soft peaks form. Set aside. Combine egg yolks, sugar, and salt and beat well. Add sour cream and flour and beat thoroughly. Fold in egg whites.

Spoon batter into hot oiled skillet by tablespoonsful. Brown each pancake on both sides. Serve.

5 SIDE DISHES

Baked Broccoli

1/4 cup olive oil

2 tablespoons brown sugar

1 1/2 tablespoons lemon juice

1/2 teaspoon cayenne pepper

1/2 teaspoon garlic powder

1/2 teaspoon dried oregano (optional)

1/2 teaspoon dried thyme (optional)

1 pinch salt

1 pinch fresh ground black pepper

1 pound broccoli florets (thaw first if using frozen)

Preheat oven to 350 degrees F (175 degrees C).

In a bowl, mix together the olive oil, brown sugar, lemon juice, cayenne pepper, garlic powder, oregano, thyme, salt, and black pepper until thoroughly combined. Add the broccoli florets, and toss until evenly coated with the seasoning. Spread the broccoli florets out onto an baking sheet with a rim.

Bake in the preheated oven until the broccoli is just browned on the top, 10 to 15 minutes.

Corn Dog Casserole

2 Tbsp. of butter or margarine

1 tsp. onion powder

1 1/2 lbs. of hot dogs, sliced/diced

2 eggs

1 1/2 cups milk

1/2 tsp. pepper

2 (8 oz.) boxes of Jiffy cornbread mix

2 cups shredded cheddar

2 tsp. rubbed sage (optional)

Preheat oven to 400°. Melt butter in a skillet. Saute hot dogs and onion powder until lightly browned. Set aside 1 cup. In a large bowl, mix eggs, milk, sage, and pepper. Add remaining hot dogs to the mixture. Stir in the 2 boxes of Jiffy mix and 1 1/2 cups of cheddar. Spray a 9"X13" dish with non-stick spray. Pour mixture into the dish. Top with remaining hot dogs and cheese. Bake uncovered for 20-25 minutes.

Broccoli Cheese Casserole

5 boxes frozen chopped broccoli

1 pound Velveeta cheese

Salt, black pepper, garlic powder (all to taste)

3/4 cup (1 1/2 sticks) butter or margarine

1 sleeve Ritz crackers

Cook broccoli according to directions on box. Add salt, pepper and garlic powder to taste.

Melt 1 stick butter and Velveeta cheese (careful not to burn). Add cheese mixture.

Crumble crackers and mix throughout, saving some for the top. Top casserole with remaining butter.

Bake 20–25 minutes at 350 degrees.

Green Bean Casserole

1 can condensed cream of mushroom soup

3/4 cup milk

1/8 tsp. pepper

16 oz frozen cut green beans (thawed and drained) or 2 cans cut green beans, drained

1 can French's french fried onions (2.8 oz can)

In a 1 1/2 quart casserole, mix soup, milk and pepper2. Stir in green beans and 1/2 can French's french fried onions.

Bake at 350 for 30 minutes or until hot. Stir; top with remaining onions.

Bake 5 minutes or until onions are golden brown.

Corn Pudding

1 can cream corn

1 can whole kernel corn (drained)

2 beaten eggs

1/2 cup butter (melted) or margarine

One 8 oz. container sour cream

1 box Jiffy corn bread mix

1 tablespoon sugar

Mix all ingredients together in large bowl.

Bake in 9 x 13 buttered pan at 350 degrees F for 45 minutes.

Easy Baked Beans

1/2 pound bacon, chopped

1 tsp onion flakes

2 (15 ounce) cans baked beans

1/4 cup brown sugar

1/4 cup ketchup

1/4 cup prepared mustard

Place bacon in a large, deep skillet. Cook over medium high heat until evenly brown. Drain excess oil, if desired. Stir in the beans, brown sugar, onion flakes, ketchup and mustard. Cook, stirring occasionally, until bubbly

Deviled Eggs

1 dozen eggs

2 teaspoons Dijon mustard

1/3 cup mayonnaise

1 Tbsp minced onion or shallot (optional)

1/4 teaspoon Tabasco

Salt and pepper

Paprika

First hard boil the eggs. (See how to make hard boiled eggs.) Fill up a large saucepan half-way with water and gently add the eggs. Cover the eggs with at least an inch of water. Add a teaspoon of vinegar to the water (this will help contain egg whites from leaking out if any of the shells crack while cooking). Add a pinch of salt to the water. Bring the water to a boil. Cover, and remove from heat. Let sit covered for 12-15 minutes. Drain hot water from pan and run cold water over the eggs. (At this point if you crack the egg shells while the eggs are cooling, it will make it easier to peel the shells.) Let sit in the cool water a few minutes, changing the water if necessary to keep it cool.

Peel the eggs. Using a sharp knife, slice each egg in half, lengthwise. Gently remove the yolk halves and place in a small mixing bowl. Arrange the egg white halves on a serving platter.

Using a fork, mash up the yolks and add mustard, mayonnaise, onion, Tabasco, and a sprinkling of salt and pepper. Spoon egg yolk mixture into the egg white halves. Sprinkle with paprika.

Cranberry Jello Salad

1 small and 1 big box of cherry jello

2 cans whole cranberry sauce

1 (20 oz) can crushed pineapple (drain and save juice)

8 oz cream cheese

 8 oz cool whip

Dissolve jello in 3 cups boiled water. Add canned cranberry and pineapple.

Pour into 9x13 pan. Refrigerate until set.

Whip cream cheese with cool whip and saved pineapple juice. Spread

over jello. Chill again until set. Cut into squares and serve.

Optional: Chopped pecans sprinkled on top if in stock at the dollar store

6 MAIN DISHES

Black Bean Burgers

1 can Black Beans, drained

1/2 cup flour

2 slices Bread, crumbled

1 tsp Garlic Powder

1 tsp Onion Powder

1/2 tsp Seasoned Salt

Salt and Pepper to taste

Oil for frying

In a large bowl, mash the beans until almost smooth. Add the rest of the ingredients, except the oil, adding the flour a few tablespoons at a time to combine well. Mixture will be thick.

Form bean mixture into patties, approximately ½ inch thick and fry patties in a small amount of oil until slightly firm. Add your favorite condiments and enjoy!

Cheesy Chicken & Broccoli Bake

1 pkg. (6 oz.) Stuffing Mix for Chicken

1-1/2 lb. boneless skinless chicken breasts, cut into bite-size pieces (We have also used canned chicken)

1 pkg. (16 oz.) frozen broccoli florets, thawed, drained

1 can (10-3/4 oz.) reduced-sodium condensed cream of chicken soup

1 lb. (8 oz.) VELVEETA Pasteurized Prepared Cheese Product, cut into 1/2-inch cubes

Heat oven to 400 degrees F. Prepare stuffing mix as directed on package; set aside.

Combine remaining ingredients; spoon into 13x9-inch baking dish. Top with stuffing. Bake 40 minutes or until chicken is done.

Cheesy Penne Pasta

1 (16 ounce) package dry penne pasta

4 tablespoons olive oil

1 teaspoon minced garlic

Bring a large pot of lightly salted water to a boil. Add penne pasta and cook for 8 to 10 minutes or until al dente; drain. (We also use the pasta boat in the microwave)

In small saucepan, saute garlic a small amount of oil. Combine garlic, olive oil, and pasta in a bowl. Mix in parmesan cheese

Easy Chicken Pot Pie

2 cups chicken, cooked and chopped

15 ounce can mixed vegetables, drained

2 10 ¾ ounce cans cream of chicken soup

1 cup milk

10 ounce tube refrigerated biscuits

Combine first four ingredients together, placing an ungreased 3 quart casserole dish.

Bake at 400 degrees F for 20 minutes.

While baking, slice biscuits into quarters and set aside.

Remove casserole dish from oven and stir.

Arrange biscuit pieces on top of the chicken mixture; bake until golden (about 15 minutes).

Easy Pizza Casserole

2 pouches (7.5 oz each) buttermilk biscuit mix

1 cup water

1 jar (14 oz) pizza sauce

1 package (8 oz) sliced pepperoni

2 cups shredded mozzarella cheese (8 oz)

Heat oven to 375°F. Spray 13x9-inch (3-quart) glass baking dish with cooking spray. In medium bowl, stir buttermilk biscuit mix and water until soft dough forms. Drop half of dough by spoonfuls evenly in bottom of baking dish (dough will not completely cover bottom of dish).

Drizzle about 1 cup pizza sauce over dough. Arrange 1/2 of the pepperoni slices evenly over sauce. Top with 1 cup of the cheese. Repeat layers with remaining dough, pizza sauce, pepperoni and cheese.

Bake 20 to 25 minutes or until golden brown. Cut into squares to serve.

Ham and Cheese Roll Ups

1 1/2 cups shredded Cheddar cheese (6 ounces)

1/4 cup mayonnaise or salad dressing

1/4 cup sour cream

1 can (11 ounces) whole kernel corn or whole kernel corn with red and green peppers, drained

10 flour tortillas (6 inches in diameter) 10 slices (1 ounce each) deli fully cooked ham

Mix cheese, mayonnaise, sour cream and corn.

Top each tortilla with 1 slice ham. Spread 2 tablespoons corn mixture over ham.

Hot Dog Mac & Cheese

1 pkg. (7-1/4 oz.) Macaroni & Cheese Dinner

1 cup frozen peas

4 Hot Dogs, cut into 1/2-inch-thick slices

¼ cup milk

½ cup Shredded Cheddar Cheese

PREPARE Macaroni and Cheese Dinner in large saucepan as directed on package.

ADD remaining ingredients; mix well. Simmer on medium-low heat 5 min or until heated through, stirring occasionally.

Italian Style Mac & Cheese

1 package macaroni and cheese mix

2 tablespoons butter

1 cup Italian-style bread crumbs

Preheat oven to 350*

Make macaroni and cheese according to package directions. Transfer to a medium-size baking dish or casserole dish.

Melt butter in a medium bowl on low power in the microwave. Add bread crumbs to bowl and toss to combine with butter. Sprinkle bread crumb mixture over top of macaroni and cheese. Place in oven and bake for 10 to 15 minutes, or until browned on top.

Marinara Chicken

3 boneless skinless chicken breasts, cut in half

26 oz jar marinara sauce

8 oz box spaghetti or pasta of choice

2.25 oz can sliced black olives, drained

1 bay leaf

1/4 t black pepper

1/2 t dried oregano

1/2 t dried basil

Set chicken in bottom of crock-pot. Add remaining ingredients and mix thoroughly, making sure all chicken ends up on the bottom of the slow cooker and covered by sauce. Cook, covered, for 7 hours on low.

Cook pasta per package directions; drain. Remove bay leaf, stir crock-pot mixture and serve over pasta.

Mexican Lasagna

3 Tablespoons olive oil

2 pounds ground chicken breast

2 Tablespoons chili powder

2 teaspoons ground cumin

1 cup taco sauce

1 (15-ounce) can black beans, drained

1 cup frozen corn

salt

8 (8 inch) soft corn or flour tortillas

2 1/2 cups shredded Cheddar cheese

sliced black olives for topping

Preheat oven to 425 degrees F.

Preheat a large skillet over medium high heat. Add 2 Tablespoons of the olive oil to the skillet. Add ground chicken and season with chili powder and cumin. Brown the meat (about 5 minutes). Add taco sauce, black beans and corn. Heat the mixture through then season with salt to taste. Coat a shallow baking dish with remaining Tablespoon of olive oil. Cut the tortillas in quarters for easy layering. Start with a layer of the meat mixture, then layer with tortillas and then cheese. Repeat for a second layer, ending with cheese.

Bake lasagna 12 to 15 minutes until cheese is slightly browned. Remove from oven, top with sliced black olives and serve.

Mini Pizza's

4 English Muffins

¾ cup tomato sauce or pizza sauce

½ cup grated cheese (mozzarella, parmesan sprinkle cheese)

½ tsp basil

½ tsp oregano

½ tsp parsley

¼ pound pepperoni

Spread tomato sauce on toasted muffins.

Put cheeses on muffins

Sprinkle herbs over the cheese.

Place slices of pepperoni over cheese and Broil at 500* for 2-4 minutes.

Oven Fried Chicken

1/4 cup chicken broth

3/4 cup finely crushed corn flakes

1/2 teaspoon garlic powder

1/8 teaspoon ground black pepper

1/8 teaspoon ground red pepper

1 1/4 pounds skinless, boneless chicken breast halves

Heat the oven to 400°F.

Pour the broth into a shallow bowl. Stir the corn flakes, garlic powder, black pepper and red pepper on a plate.

Dip the chicken into the broth. Coat with the corn flake mixture. Place the chicken onto a baking sheet.

Bake for 20 minutes or until the chicken is cooked through.

Sloppy Joe Casserole

1 1/2 pounds ground beef

1 can (15 1/2 ounces) sloppy joe sauce

2 cups (8 ounces) shredded cheddar cheese

2 cups baking mix (Bisquick)

2 eggs, lightly beaten

1 cup milk

In a large skillet, cook beef over medium heat until no longer pink. Drain.

Stir sloppy joe sauce into beef. Mix well.

Transfer mixture to a lightly greased 13x9 baking dish. Sprinkle cheese over top.

Combine the biscuit mix, eggs and milk in a large bowl until just until blended.

Pour biscuit mixture over the cheese in casserole.

Bake, uncovered, at 400° for 25 minutes or until golden brown.

Slow Cooker Chicken & Stuffing

4 cups of cooked chicken

1 box of stuffing mix, chicken flavor

2 eggs

1 cup water (or chicken broth for more flavor)

1½ cups milk

Combine chicken and dry stuffing mix. Place in a greased 4-5 quart slow cooker.

Beat eggs, water (or broth), and milk together in a bowl. Pour over chicken and stuffing.

Cover and cook on high for 2-3 hours.

Crock Pot Creamy Chicken & Rice

1 c uncooked white rice

1 chicken, cut in parts

103/4 oz can cream of celery soup

103/4 oz can cream of mushroom soup

1 package dry onion soup mix

1/2 c water

Combine water, soups and dry onion soup mix together. Mix
about 1/2 of mixture with rice and layer on bottom of a 3.5 quart
or larger crock pot. Layer chicken on top of rice. Pour
remaining soup mixture over chicken. Cover and cook for 7-8
hours on low, or until chicken is cooked through.

Tater-Tot Casserole

1 lb lean ground beef

1 (10 1/2 ounce) can condensed cream of celery or cream of mushroom soup (undiluted)

1 16oz package frozen tater tots

1 cup shredded cheddar cheese

salt & pepper

Preheat oven to 375 *.

Brown ground beef. season with salt & pepper.

In a casserole dish, combine ground beef mixture & cream soup.

Top mixture with tater tots.

Bake , uncovered, for 30-40 minutes till bubbly and Tots are golden brown.

Remove from oven & top with cheese, return to oven until melted.

7 DESSERT

Aunt Minnie's Oatmeal Crisp Cake

1 cup oatmeal (quick)

1 cup of flour

1 stick margarine

1 cup brown sugar

1 can pie filling (cherry & apple are our favorite)

Put everything except pie filling into a bowl and work with hands until crumbly. Spread 2/3 of crumbs on bottom of pan, be sure bottom is covered. Spread pie filling next. Put rest of crumbs on top.

Bake at 350 degrees in a 9 X 13 pan for approximately 45 minutes.

Recipe can be doubled and baked in a 15 1/2 X 10 X 1 inch pan for approximately 1 1/2 hours at 350 degrees.

Baking time may vary depending on your oven. If using a glass pan decrease oven heat to 325 degrees.

Boiled Cookies

2 Cups Sugar

½ Cup Milk

¼ lb butter or margarine

4 heaping tbs cocoa

2 ½ Cups Oatmeal

¼ Cup Chopped walnuts (optional)

2 tsp vanilla

½ Cup Peanut Butter

In a saucepan cook sugar, milk and cocoa until melted.

Bring to a boil and continue stirring for 1 ½ minutes.

(boiling for 1 ½ minutes is crucial to success!)

Remove from heat.

Add peanut butter, vanilla, nuts, and oatmeal stirring quickly.

Immediately spoon cookies onto wax paper to set or in a greased

pan to make squares.

Carmel Popcorn Bars

1 bag (3.5 oz) microwave popcorn (any variety), popped

1 cup coarsely crushed peanut brittle (6 oz)

1 bag (14 oz) caramels

1 tablespoon water

1/4 teaspoon vanilla

Butter bottom and sides of 13x9-inch pan. Remove and discard unpopped kernels from popped popcorn.

In large bowl, mix popcorn and peanut brittle. In 4-cup microwavable measuring cup, microwave caramels and water uncovered on High 2 to 4 minutes, stirring every minute, until smooth. Stir in vanilla.

Pour over popcorn mixture; toss until evenly coated. Press in pan with buttered hands. Let stand about 30 minutes or until set. For 24 bars, cut into 6 rows by 4 rows with wet knife.

Chocolate Peanut Butter Fudge

Place in a 2 quart pan

1 cup brown sugar

1 cup white sugar

1 cup miniature marshmallows

1/4 cup cocoa

1/2 cup evaporated milk

Bring to a boil on medium heat while stirring constantly until marshmallows are completely melted. Remove from heat source.

Stir in 1 cup smooth or crunchy peanut butter & a teaspoon of vanilla until well blended. Pour into a buttered pan (foil pan from graham cracker crust is just the right size-your choice.

Fudge can be left solid and cut when needed. Can be frozen.

Cream Puff Cake

1 Cup Water

1 Stick Margarine

Bring water and margarine to a boil. Remove from heat and add

1 Cup flour. Beat well and mix in 4 eggs, one at a time.

Spread in greased 9x13 pan and bake at 450* for 20 min. Then lower the temp to 350*

and bake for 15 min. This layer will not bake evenly.Mash down bubbles after removing

from oven and cool.

Filling:

1 (8oz) cream cheese

2 small boxes Instant pudding (any flavor)

3 cups milk

Beat cream cheese and milk alternating with pudding until all is mixed.

Put on completely cooled cake.

Top with large container of cool whip. If the dollar store has chocolate syrup you may drizzle that over the top!

Microwave Peanut Butter Fudge

12 oz. semi-sweet chocolate chips

12 oz. peanut butter

14 oz. sweetened condensed milk

In a 1-1/2 quart microwave-proof bowl, melt chocolate and peanut butter on high power for 3 minutes. Stir well.

Add milk and stir until well blended.

Pour mixture into 8x8 dish lined with waxed paper. Refrigerate to chill.

Flourless Peanut Butter Cookies

Makes 18 cookies.

1 cup natural peanut butter

1 cup sugar

1 large egg, lightly beaten

1 teaspoon vanilla extract

Coarse sea salt

Preheat the oven to 350 degrees F and place racks in the upper and lower third of the oven.

In a medium bowl, mix the peanut butter, sugar, egg and vanilla until well combined. Spoon 1 tablespoon of mixture about 1 inch apart onto ungreased baking sheets. Flatten the mounds with the tines of a fork, making a crosshatch pattern on the cookies. Sprinkle coarse salt on top of the cookies.

Bake until golden around edges, about 10 minutes, switching the position of the pans halfway thorough baking. Transfer to racks to cool. Repeat with the remaining dough.

Lemon Cake

1 pkg yellow cake mix

1pkg instant lemon pudding

¾ cup water

¾ cup veg oil

4 eggs

Mix all and pour in 9x13 ungreased cake pan.

Bake at 350 for 35 minutes. Make Icing while cake cools.

Icing

1/3 cup orange juice

2 cup sugar

2 tbs warm water

2 tbs butter or margarine

Mix icing ingredients together.

Poke cake all over top (end of wooden spoon works great)

Pour Icing over the cooled cake.

Oatmeal Cookies

¾ Cup Shortening

1 Cup packed brown sugar

½ Cup sugar

1 egg

¼ water

1 tsp vanilla

Mix the above ingredients well.

Next mix together:

 3 Cups Oatmeal

1 Cup Flour

1 tsp salt

½ tsp baking soda

Stir all ingredients together. Drop dough by tsp on greased

cookie sheet. Bake at 350 for 12- 14 minutes til lightly brown.

(I like adding in butterscotch or chocolate chips if the dollar store has them)

Also you can chill or freeze the dough if you don't want to bake them

all at once or are using a tabletop oven.

Peanut Butter Cake

1 stick butter

1 cup water

½ cup peanut butter

½ cup oil

Bring to a boil.

Then add:

2 cups flour

2 cups sugar

2 eggs

1tsp vanilla

½ cup milk

1 tsp baking soda

Pour into un-greased cake pan. Bake at 350* for 25-30 min.

While cake is cooling mix up the following for Frosting:

In saucepan bring a ½ cup milk and ½ cup peanut butter to a boil.

Add 1 tsp vanilla and slowly mix in a pound of

powdered sugar. Mix well and pour over cake.

Pistachio Salad

1 Pkg Instant pistachio pudding

20 oz can crushed pineapple

1 ½ cup mini marshmallows

1 lg container of cool whip

Chopped walnuts optional

Mix first three ingredients together and let stand. Add cool whip and

Refrigerate.

Pumpkin Yellow Cake

1 large Can Pumpkin

3 eggs

1 Cup Sugar

1 Cup Milk

Dash Salt

Mix all ingredients and pour in ungreased 9x13 pan. Sprinkle 1 cup

Yellow Cake mix on top. Drizzle ½ cup melted butter on cake mix.

(Optional Chopped nuts on top to garnish)

Cover with foil and bake at 350* for 45 min. Remove foil and bake another

15 minutes.

Quick Chocolate Frosting

¼ cup melted shortening or butter

1/3 cup cocoa

¼ tsp salt

1/3 cup milk

1 ½ tsp vanilla

3 1/3 Cup powdered sugar

Combine butter, cocoa, and salt. Add in vanilla and milk using a mixer.

Add powdered sugar in three parts. Mix until smooth and creamy.

(If frosting is too thick just use a little milk to thin to desired texture)

Grandma's No Fail Pie Crust

4 cups Flour

1 ¾ cup Crisco (or other brand Shortening)

2tsp. salt

1 Tbs Sugar

Combine above until size of crumbly peas.

Mix the following together and add to flour mixture:

½ cup water

1 egg

1Tbs vinegar

Mix all together and form into a ball. Chill before rolling out to make the dough more manageable.

Makes 2 average double crusted pies. Can be kept in the refrigerator for 2- 3 days or frozen for later use.

PS.. Besides making pies. You may also roll out dough using flour and place on a cookie sheet. Top with sugar & cinnamon. Bake at 375* until brown around the edges. Its flakey and good!

Sweet Chili Brownies

1 box (18.3-ounce) fudge brownie mix

2/3 cup vegetable oil

2 eggs

1/4 cup chocolate milk

3 tablespoons chili powder

2 tablespoons chopped canned jalapenos

1 teaspoon ground cinnamon

Powdered sugar

Preheat oven to 350* In a large mixing bowl, stir together all ingredients, except powdered sugar. Spread batter evenly into greased (cooking spray) 9x13 pan.

Bake for 24 to 26 minutes

Cool completely and dust with powdered sugar

Texas Sheet Cake

2 stick butter

1 cup water

4 tbs cocoa

Bring to boil and add:

2 cups flour

2 cups sugar

Dash salt

2 eggs

½ cup sour cream

1 tsp baking soda

Mix this batter and pour into a 10x15 sheet pan. Bake at 375

for 20 to 30 minutes.

Icing

In a cooking pot mix the following:

 1 stick butter

4 tbs cocoa

6 tbs milk

Bring to boil and and add 1 pound powdered sugar and 1 tsp vanilla.

Frost cooled cake.

Sprinkle with chopped walnuts if desired.

Diet Cup-Cake

(From The Cover)

1 Box any flavor box of cake mix (pick a favorite flavor)

1 Box Angel Food cake mix

Mix the two together and store in a sealed container or plastic bag until you want to make a Cup-Cake.

To make the Cup-Cake Put 3tbs of the mixture into a microwavable mug or bowl. Add 2 tbs. water into mug and mix.

Put in the microwave for 1 minute and you have a cupcake! You may ice the cupcake or use fat free whipped topping . I often double the recipe which will fill the mug when its done cooking.

*You may put fruit such as peaches in the mix to give added flavor.

ABOUT THE AUTHORS

When Colleen Timko and Meranda Hendricks opened the Hound Hut, a dog daycare and grooming facility in Gahanna Ohio, little did they know that they would spend long hours every day getting this new business off the ground.

Soon it became evident that there was little time for grocery shopping so they found themselves shopping at their next door neighbor which happened to be a dollar store.

Two years have passed and they have compiled a book of their favorite recipes using items purchased from the dollar store. They still try to find the time to shop the farmers market when it is in season but know that a great meal is as close as their next door neighbor!

www.ingramcontent.com/pod-product-compliance
Lightning Source LLC
Chambersburg PA
CBHW060702030426
42337CB00017B/2717